Succession:
Are You Ready?

MEMO TO THE CEO

Authored by leading experts and examining issues of special urgency, the books in the Memo to the CEO series are tailored for today's time-starved executives. Concise, focused, and solutions-oriented, each book explores a critical management challenge and offers authoritative counsel, provocative points of view, and practical insight.

Climate Change: What's Your Business Strategy?
by Andrew J. Hoffman and John G. Woody

Five Future Strategies You Need Right Now
by George Stalk, the Boston Consulting Group

High Performance with High Integrity
by Ben Heineman, former General Counsel
of General Electric

*Lessons from Private Equity Any Company
Can Use*
by Orit Gadiesh and Hugh MacArthur,
Bain & Company, Inc.

Manage the Media
(Don't Let the Media Manage You)
by William J. Holstein, award-winning writer for
the *New York Times*, *Fortune*, and *Barron's*

Reward Systems: Does Yours Measure Up?
by Steve Kerr, former CLO of General Electric
and Goldman Sachs

Strategic Alliances: Three Ways to Make Them Work
by Steve Steinhilber, Vice President of Strategic
Alliances at Cisco Systems

MEMO TO THE CEO

Succession: Are You Ready?

Marshall Goldsmith

Harvard Business Press

Boston, Massachusetts

Copyright 2009 Harvard Business School Publishing Corporation
All rights reserved
Printed in the United States of America
12 11 10 09 08   5 4 3 2 1

ISBN 978-1-4221-1823-8

Library- of- Congress cataloging information available

The paper used in this publication meets the requirements of the American
National Standard for Permanence of Paper for Publications and Documents
in Libraries and Archives Z39.48-1992.

Contents

Contents

Note to the Reader

In writing *Succession: Are You Ready?* I have imagined myself trying to help the CEO of a major corporation who is nearing the end of his or her career navigate the succession process in a manner that is beneficial for the CEO, the successor, and the organization. *Succession: Are You Ready?* is written in the form of a series of short, sequential memos that are intended to provide practical "real-world" advice to this CEO.

While the book is written as my correspondence with a major CEO, much of the content applies to *any* leader who is going through the transition process. In fact, after reviewing the manuscript, I believe that entrepreneurial leaders (and especially founders) can perhaps benefit from these suggestions even more than corporate CEOs.

My personal area of expertise is helping successful leaders achieve positive, lasting change in behavior: for themselves, their people, and their teams. Therefore, the entire book is focused on the human, or *behavioral*, elements of transition. I fully understand that strategic or technical issues in succession can be just as important or, in some cases, even more important than behavioral concerns. This book does not address these issues not because they are unimportant. This book does not address these issues because I do not feel qualified to speak as an expert on these topics.

What is this book designed to do?

This book has been written to help leaders:

- *Prepare for transition.* Transition is a process that every leader will eventually face. While a few handle it very well, many do not handle it well at all. Very few leaders appreciate how challenging transition is going to be for them. Hopefully, the suggestions in this book will help leaders prepare to leave their positions with class and dignity.
- *Choose a successor.* While these "memos" do not cover many of the elements of leadership succession (such as functional experience), they can provide help in understanding the behavioral dynamics of the succession process. They can also help leaders face the reality that sometimes even qualified successors are not going to get the job.
- *Coach your successor.* The behavioral coaching process described in this book has been successfully

implemented with thousands of leaders, at all levels, around the world. This type of coaching has one goal: to help the leader being coached achieve positive change in desired behavior as determined by key stakeholders. This process is about building relationships—and it works on issues that are behavioral, when the person (being coached) is given a fair chance and if the person is willing to try. At the executive level, the vast majority of coaching needs to fit this description.

• *Pass the baton.* My mentor, friend, and hero, Frances Hesselbein, has noted, "Successful transition is the last act of a great leader." Far too many leaders (as well as athletes, actors, and other professionals) just cannot let go. They hang around until they are asked to leave—then they have nowhere to go. Hopefully, this book will help leaders "move on" to a next phase of life that provides meaning, contribution, and happiness.

There are many important questions about succession that this book will not answer. For example, the focus of these memos is helping the CEO develop one successor. The memos do not deal with the issue of whether the CEO should have a "horse race" and develop several potential successors at once. While the book does not talk about using the coaching process for more than one person—the process can readily be adopted for this application. Leadership development should be an ongoing process that is part of life for leaders at all levels—not just CEO candidates.

This book is not intended to be a human resources manual that outlines all of the details of succession planning. Others have already written books on this topic that are far better than I could hope to author. For example, *Succession: Are You Ready?* doesn't deal with compensation, stock options, and myriad other HR concerns that may come into play.

This book is written for leaders who have the good fortune to be leaving on their own terms—and not being told to leave by the board. I recognize that, in many succession situations, this is not the case. Unfortunately, "planned departures" are less common than they used to be. These memos are for leaders who have earned the privilege—through achieving results and good luck—of leaving by choice.

My suggestion for you, the reader, is to apply what you are reading in the context of your own life. You don't have to be a CEO to face the challenges of transition and succession. Hopefully, this book will help you to plan for *your* next transition in life—and help you to help others get ready for succession.

Preface: Memo to the CEO

For three decades, I have had the privilege of working with over one hundred major CEOs and their management teams. In this memo I will share with you—a CEO who is nearing the end of his or her tenure—what I have learned from my years of practice in executive coaching. Hopefully, you can learn from my experience with other CEOs and not repeat some of the classic mistakes that I have observed over the years.

After you leave your role as CEO of this company, you may wish to coach other leaders. This memo should also help you in coaching entrepreneurs, executives, or professionals who are preparing for their career transitions. While some of our discussion relates exclusively to CEOs, most of this memo is applicable to any high-level professional transition.

From my observation, much of what has been written about CEO succession has little to do with the personal drama that actually transpires when it comes time to hand off the baton of leadership.

"Academic" literature generally ignores the fact that CEOs—and their successors—are *human beings*. Very little of what is written deals with "soft" personal issues like *relationships*, *self-interest*, *ego*, or (God forbid) *feelings*!

Leadership succession is usually presented as a dry, "check-the-boxes" process during which seemingly robotic executives are only concerned with buzzwords like *strategic fit*, *core competencies*, and *long-term shareholder value*. These writings make an implicit assumption that CEO succession is completely impersonal, objective, and rational.

Wrong!

In actual practice, the process of getting ready for succession is often influenced by *emotions* as much as it is influenced by *logic*.

Almost no occupational group is more personally identified with their jobs than CEOs. When you are introduced, you are referred to as the CEO of your company. After a while, this is not just *what you do*—it becomes a very large part of *who you are.* At the CEO level, the transition process is far from impersonal—it is extremely personal!

One of my coaching clients described her emotional reaction, when she finally faced the reality of leaving her job, to a group of fellow executives from different companies: "I finally realized that my job had become my best friend." She sighed, "It's very hard to leave your best friend." I watched the expressive face of this fantastic leader as she shared her personal feelings about leaving. The CEOs in the room were hanging on her every word.

"It seemed like I was getting promoted every few years. I loved the company, my coworkers, and our customers. Going to work was always a joy for me," she smiled. Her face changed expression as she went on, "The time just flew by—and then one day it was time to leave. It hurt."

The transition process will not only be "personal" for you. It will be "personal" for your successor, your other executives, your board, and all the other stakeholders whose lives you impact.

In the old *Star Trek* series, Leonard Nimoy played the role of Mr. Spock, a pointy-eared leader from Vulcan, a planet whose citizens prided themselves on pure objective logic and the absence of any "illogical" emotions. Many management texts are written as if the executives they are describing are Vulcans. Unless some clever plastic surgeons from Beverly Hills are doing ear reconstructions, I have never met a Vulcan CEO here on planet Earth!

A reason for this memo is to prepare you for the *human* side of CEO succession. You—like all of the other CEOs that I have met—appear to be a human being, not a cleverly designed android. Assuming that this observation is correct, you are likely to be subject to many of the same crazy, emotional, nonrational hopes and fears that plague the rest of humanity.

I am definitely not an expert on strategy, execution, or the "business" side of business. My PhD is in organizational behavior and my area of expertise involves the *behavioral* side of leadership. All of my suggestions will be limited to issues involving human behavior.

My goal for you is to get through the transition process in the most positive manner possible. I would like you to maintain your dignity (many don't), enjoy your final year or so in the office, and put your successor in a position where he or she will have a great chance of winning.

I would like to help you help your successor develop the leadership skills and key relationships that he or she will need to succeed. The coaching process that I will describe has been proven to work—as a tool for achieving positive, lasting change in behavior, building stakeholder relationships, and increasing leadership effectiveness.

You are the CEO, not me. In this memo, I will do my best to give you suggestions based on my years of experience. At the end of the day, the "ownership" of how you manage this process has to come from you. Think about all of my suggestions, weigh them against your own years of executive experience, and choose a path for the development of your successor that fits your own unique background and skill.

PART I

Preparing Yourself

1   Slowing Down

You are carrying the baton in a very special relay race. As the CEO, you have been given the privilege of carrying the baton of leadership. If you do a great job of carrying this baton, your organization may last long beyond your tenure. You have been given this extraordinary baton for only a short segment of your organization's life. At some point in time, you will need to hand it off to another leader who will take your place. You will be amazed at how quickly this time passes! Will you—and your successor—be ready for this handoff?

Passing the Baton of Leadership

Unlike a relay race in the Olympics, your relay has some very different rules. To begin with, if your organization continues to prosper, a series of baton carriers can help keep your company running for years and years! Rather than having a fixed amount of distance to carry the baton, you may have an indeterminate amount of time. Unlike in the Olympics, you may be given a large say in determining when the handoff will occur—and you may help determine who the new baton carrier will be.

In your relay, your team's competitors never stop. While some of your competitors may stumble and disappear from the race, others may leap from the stands and start running—at any time! While looking ahead at the track in front of you, you have to simultaneously look in all directions for future competitors.

In this race, you—as the baton carrier—need to balance two priorities that often, if not usually, conflict with each other. On one hand, you need to produce short-term, quarterly results. While analysts may forgive a few bad quarters, if you have too many missteps, you will quickly be out of the race. You need to try to win as many quarters as you can. On the other hand, you need to do what is in the best long-term interest of your organization. If you don't do what is right for the organization in the long term, your company will eventually be out of the race—and you will have failed in your responsibility as its baton carrier.

One positive aspect of your role as a CEO is that while carrying the baton of leadership, you can begin to prepare your successor for the handoff. In a relay race, in preparing for the handoff, one runner has to speed up while the other has to slow down. You can help ensure that your successor is up to speed as you begin to slow down to hand over the baton.

This memo is designed to help you (1) slow down and make the handoff of leadership and (2) coach your chosen successor to speed up and successfully carry the baton.

In the Olympic relays, a large audience is watching. They cheer as the handoff is made. Each new baton carrier brings new hope. If their team is behind, the crowd hopes that the new runner will close the gap. If their team is ahead, they hope that the new runner will expand the lead.

As you carry the baton of CEO leadership, a varied audience is watching your every stride. The members of your audience care even more about your performance than the people in the stands care about the performance of Olympic athletes. Stockholders are frantically "checking your time" to make sure that they are getting a return on their invested dollars—and wondering if you can keep delivering. Analysts are counting to make sure that you are meeting commitments—and pondering your chances for success in the next lap of the race. Customers are watching to make sure that you deliver value—and wondering what you have in store for them in the future. Employees are critically reviewing your actions to make sure that your deeds match your words—and considering if your leadership will keep your organization their career choice. Competitors are looking for signs of exhaustion—and hoping that you will fade.

As in the Olympics, everyone who is counting on you will cheer wildly if you run a great leg and make a successful handoff. Unlike in the Olympics, you won't get to stand on a podium at the end of a race, wear a medal, hear applause, and listen to your country's national anthem.

After the handoff, you will quickly disappear from view. Everyone will start cheering for the next baton carrier.

What will be your legacy? If you do a great job in developing your successor, part of your legacy will be that you were a leader who took the high road and worked to ensure that your organization would become even more successful after your departure. You will be viewed as a leader who helped ensure that the values of the organization lived on after you were no longer there.

As you carry the CEO baton, you need to get ready for your own departure. You need to get ready for succession. You may well think that this will be easy. You will be wrong. It is almost always tougher than you can imagine.

If you are not forced to hand off the baton before you want to, you will be tempted to just keep on running. If you are ahead, and pulling away from the pack, you will hear the crowd. They won't want you to quit. They will be screaming—go, go, go! You will be feeling great. Everyone will love you. Why in the world would you want to hand off the baton now? It feels like a magic baton that is propelling your team to glory.

It is easy to fall in love with the baton of leadership. Whenever this happens, it is almost impossible to let it go.

If you fall behind on your leg of the relay, you won't want to give up. If you hand off the baton, you may end up being called "the runner who blew the race." Your competitive drive won't want to let that happen. You just know that you can beat the runner in front of you, if you are given a little more time.

Passing the baton is the final challenge of great leadership. If you do it poorly, or even drop the baton, you may do grave damage to your organization.

If you do it well, and if you have a lot of class, you can then sit in the stands and applaud as your successor races ahead. You will smile as you watch your successor's face—remember carrying the baton—and look up the track for the next baton carrier, who is eagerly waiting for the handoff.

Are you ready for succession?

The answer to this question can be a key factor in determining your organization's success after you leave!

"Stopping" May Not Be an Option

People live a lot longer than they used to. If you leave the CEO role in your sixties (most do), you may well have twenty or more "good years" ahead of you. Today, when people, like you, have the ambition, drive, and energy to achieve great success in any field, it is very unlikely that your ambition, drive, and energy will just stop when you change jobs.

I have never met a successful CEO in my life who was lazy. CEOs, like you, are incredibly ambitious and work extremely hard. In spite of some grumbling about "how tough the job is," the great chief executives who I know love their work.

Unless you are about to die when you make the transition, your drive is not going to go away. You may think that you want to just "rest and relax." According to the "retired" CEOs I have met, your desire to rest and relax won't last very long. One retired executive groaned, "After the third cruise, they start to get *really* boring!"

The prospects of sleeping late, living on the beach, improving their golf scores, going on cruises, and playing all day hold almost no allure for the great leaders who I have known. You have plenty of money. If you really wanted to "stop," you would have stopped by now.

Along with rest and relaxation, another favorite myth is "lots of quality time with my family."

You have been working almost continuously for years. For better or worse, your family has been able to survive without you at home. Don't delude yourself into believing that they really want you around all of the time. If you are married, this may be your spouse's greatest nightmare!

One top military officer shared his experience. "My wife said that she was looking forward to spending lots of time with me. One day, after a few months of 'retirement,' I was in the kitchen alphabetizing the cans. To my amazement, she didn't really seem to care if baked beans should be filed under BA for 'baked' or BE for 'beans.' On the contrary, she reminded me that this was not the military, that I was not her 'officer,' and that it was time for me to find something else to do—since I was driving her crazy."

Another former CEO laughed as he remembered his "retirement."

My kids were grown up and living their own lives. They quickly tired of my "visits." My wife got so tired of me that she got a job in a dress store—just to get out of the house. One day I had been watching TV by myself. A delivery guy came by to drop off a package. It was his last stop, so I invited him to come in for a cup of coffee. We had a very interesting conversation about life. After he left, I thought, "What a great conversation. That was the highlight of my week." Then I looked into the mirror. I hadn't shaved for three days. I had been watching junk TV. With a shock I realized what I had just said, "The highlight of my week was having a cup of coffee with the delivery guy." As a CEO, I may have had some bad weeks, but I never had a week so boring that coffee with delivery people was a highlight. I got another job the next day.

As you slow down to hand off the baton of leadership to your successor, you should have less to do at work. Let him start running the place! I have an important suggestion: use this time to start planning something exciting to do for the rest of your life. You will probably have too much drive and ambition to be a successful "retiree."

Making Peace with Slowing Down

One of the most common fears of CEOs who are getting ready to slow down and pass the baton of leadership is, "If I announce my successor in advance, isn't there a danger that I will just become a *lame duck*? I certainly wouldn't want that to happen!" Almost every executive goes through this dialogue as part of the challenge of slowing down. This fear often results in postponement of the succession announcement until the last minute—and inhibits what could have been a much smoother transition process.

When it is approaching time to leave, face reality—you *will* become a lame duck! Attention will immediately shift to your successor. Her vision for the future of the company will mean more than yours. If you disapprove of executive team members' ideas, they will just wait it out and resell the same ideas to your successor. People will start sucking up to her—in the same way they used to suck up to you.

Make peace with being a lame duck—before it actually happens—and your life, your successor's life, and the lives of the executive team members will be a lot better.

One of my favorite CEO clients actually bought a stuffed duck and wrapped up one leg—to represent

11

the fact that he was a lame duck. He brought the duck to a few meetings. His direct reports and successor thought that this was hilarious. It broke the ice about a potentially awkward topic and put the obvious fact of his upcoming departure on the table. He was at my home recently and shared this duck story with other chief executives who were facing transition. They loved it!

Be a happy and productive lame duck. Being a lame duck doesn't have to be all bad. Use this period to coach your successor (behind the scenes). Begin the transfer of power before you have to. Support your successor however you can. Build her confidence.

Involve your successor in all important decisions and, to the degree humanly possible, make sure that she agrees with your long-term strategies—*before* they are announced. Remember, she is the person who is going to have to live with these strategies for the next few years—and make them work.

If you want to be a great lame duck, make those tough, unpopular decisions that you know are good for the company. Don't worry about "finishing on a great note." Be more focused on putting your successor in a position where *she* will succeed than finishing in a way that will make *you* look good.

One of the greatest CEOs who I have ever met (in the pharmaceutical industry) made a series of long-term strategic investments in his final year. These investments hurt the short-term performance of the company and negatively impacted the stock price. In the long term, these investments paid huge dividends, benefited the company, and helped his successor look like a hero. This leader was more concerned about the long-term success of the organization than bragging about how much the stock price had gone up on his watch. This type of class and self-sacrifice is, unfortunately, far too rare.

Your final year will be your last chance to "do what is right" for the long-term benefit of the company. Use it wisely!

On the personal side, letting go can have some advantages. Go home a little earlier. Spend more time with the family you may have neglected in the past. Go to your grandkids' baseball games once in a while. Reacquaint yourself with your spouse.

Most importantly, start getting ready for the rest of your life. Spend more and more time on finding a new team (or teams) to lead—and getting ready to pick up the baton of leadership in a new race.

As you look at the transition process, contemplate figure 1-1.

At the beginning of the transition process, you should be running at full speed. Almost all of your focus has to be on leading the company, with a little

FIGURE 1-1

Effectively letting go

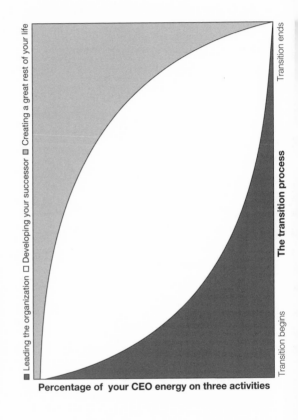

■ Leading the organization □ Developing your successor ■ Creating a great rest of your life

Transition begins   **The transition process**   Transition ends

Percentage of your CEO energy on three activities

on developing your successor, and not much on creating the rest of your life.

In the middle of the transition process, you should begin to slow down. While you are still working on leading the company, you are deeply involved in developing your successor, and you begin focusing on creating the rest of your life.

At the end of the process, you will need to stop leading the company, be available (only if asked) to work on developing your successor, and primarily focus on creating the rest of your life.

While figure 1-1 illustrates a process that theoretically *could* happen, figure 1-2 illustrates a process that actually *does* happen, and far too often. In figure 1-2 the leader becomes focused on leading the company until the bitter end, spends little time in developing his successor, and puts almost no effort into creating the rest of his life.

My advice is simple. If you want to do a great job in creating a great transition, look more like the leader in figure 1-1—less like the leader in figure 1-2.

FIGURE 1-2

Trouble letting go

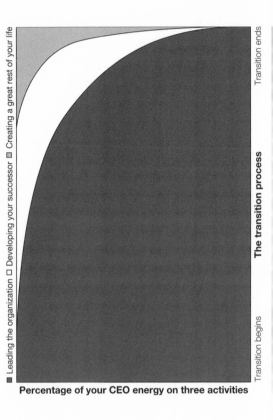

■ Leading the organization □ Developing your successor ▨ Creating a great rest of your life

Transition begins — **The transition process** — Transition ends

Percentage of your CEO energy on three activities

2   Letting Go and Moving On

If you are like many CEOs—you may start laughing as you read some of the examples in this memo—you may be remembering how crazy *other* executives acted when it was time for them to leave. Personal difficulties with transition are very easy to observe in others, but they are very hard to see in the mirror.

Almost all of the leaders who I have met assure me that *they* will be different. They confidently assert that *they* will have no problems letting go. You are probably delusional enough to believe that *you* too will be different. Take my word for it: while your desire for uniqueness may be theoretically possible, it is statistically unlikely.

Letting Go Is Hard to Do

In getting ready for your transition to "life after being the CEO," make peace with the fact that it is probably going to be very hard for you to just let go—and get on with the rest of your life. CEOs who realistically face the personal challenges of transition are much better prepared to leave than those who chronically deny the difficulty of leaving.

While you, as a CEO, have to face an enormous amount of work, pressure, and grief, let's be honest here—the job does come with a few pretty nice benefits! Each of these benefits can make you, as the chief executive, want to keep on leading—and can make it hard to let go.

Wealth

When it is time for you to leave, you will have more money than you will ever spend. One positive side of being a CEO in the 2000s is that you are rich. With very few exceptions, the CEOs who I meet don't actually care about money in terms of needing more or even wanting to buy things. They are not interested in showing off their possessions. Many plan to give most of their money away to their favorite charities. There are no material items that they want—and can buy—that have not already been bought. On the other hand, money can easily become a sort of personal "scorecard."

You may not think that it will be hard for you to walk away from making so much money. You may be surprised. One retired leader reported, "In my entire career, I always made *more* money in the present year than in the year before. I always assumed that I would make even more next year! I took it for granted. I didn't make a big deal of it, but I always 'counted the numbers.' When I realized that I was going to make a lot *less* money, I felt kind of ashamed—like I had failed. Although this doesn't seem logical, it is still the way that I felt."

Perquisites

After a few years, the perks that come with being a CEO are almost taken for granted. Flying around in the company jet, having access that most people never dream of, going to games in the company box and being supported by a dedicated professional staff are part of your daily life. When you leave the job, many of these perks go away—and you may be surprised how much you miss them.

A surprising number of retired chief executives report that it is difficult for them to adjust to standing in airport security lines, waiting for delayed flights, and eating airplane food. When retired CEOs are asked what they miss about not being a CEO, more than you would imagine mention the company jet.

Almost every retired CEO who I know misses having a personal assistant. Face it: this is the person who kept your life together for years! You are probably incapable of doing a lot of assignments that your assistant takes for granted. I have a suggestion. Get a personal assistant after you retire. You can afford it. This way you will decrease the odds of embarrassing yourself by showing the world you cannot do tasks that others have been doing for years. You will also free up your time to do work that is personally rewarding for you—and that makes a contribution to others.

Status

CEOs, like you, learn to live with amazing amounts of status. After a while, it just seems to be part of who you are. None of the great top officers that I have known have any desire to act like big shots or come off as arrogant or superior to others. They adapt well to their status and don't abuse it.

On the other hand, one of the great fears of any megasuccessful, well-known person is becoming a "used to be." Instead of being introduced as the CEO, you will be introduced as the person who "used to be the CEO." It isn't the same. To be honest, it isn't even close.

After you have retired, instead of looking at you with admiration, the ambitious young people you meet may be looking around the room for someone more significant to talk to. In the words of the Eagles'

"New Kid in Town"—*They will never forget you till somebody new comes along.*

Make peace with your loss of status in advance. Learn to enjoy the process of others' striving to get ahead. If you cannot make peace with losing status, don't retire!

Power

When I asked one executive what he had learned about leadership since becoming a CEO, he laughed and replied, "My suggestions become orders. If I want them to become orders, they are orders. If I don't want them to become orders, they are still orders. No matter how open I try to be, as the CEO of a multibillion-dollar corporation, I don't make suggestions. I give orders."

Many CEOs won't admit it, but most studies indicate that they have a higher need for power than most other human beings. Incredible power can be hard to give away.

Power can simply be defined as the potential to influence. CEOs love to get big results. It is hard to get huge projects completed without power. Throughout their careers, leaders experience an increase in power *gradually*. Over the years, as you move from position to position into higher levels of authority, you get more and more power. In sharp contrast, when you leave the role, you may lose power *suddenly*.

One executive reported, "It was like falling off a cliff. My loss of power, *'They're not bothering to return my phone calls.'* When I was the CEO, my phone calls always got returned—immediately!"

Let's stop and review what you may be giving up so far: money, perks, status, and power. You begin to get the picture. While the *theory* of stepping down from the CEO role is easy, the *practice* of letting go can be a little painful!

It can be amusing to listen to people gossip about chief executives, with apparent shock, and gasp, "I am *amazed* that anyone—who made it to the level of CEO—could have made that mistake!"

Have you ever read a history book before? Is there any evidence in the history of the world that shows when human beings are given incredible amounts of money, perks, status, and power, they begin to act completely sane and rational? I have never read that book.

Face it: you may be a CEO, but you are still a human being. Millions of leaders throughout history have had trouble letting go of money, status, perks, and power. If you cannot make peace with giving up some of this stuff, you will never be able to make a smooth handoff.

Relationships

If you make a chart of how you have spent your time for the past few years, you will find that you have spent far more time with the people at work than you have with your friends and family members. You and your coworkers have been through a lot together. Most of your success has been caused by them. Their success has been heavily influenced by you.

As a CEO, you personally *like* the vast majority of your close coworkers. If you didn't like them, they would not be your close coworkers. Along with being fellow employees, they have almost become your family. It can be hard to leave the "friends and family" at work who you have grown so close to over the years. The more you have been through together, the harder it can be to leave.

Happiness

Deep down inside, the great leaders who I have met love being CEOs. They love leading people and leading organizations. They love the challenge and they love their work. They look forward to getting up in the morning and facing the new day. They have the incredible energy that comes from loving what they do.

If retiring and playing golf were really more fun than being a CEO, you would already be retired and you wouldn't be reading this memo. As you face transition, you will need to look for new ways to find the happiness that came with being a chief executive.

Meaning

Being a CEO matters! Your actions have direct impact on people, products, and your world. Your work is not trivial—it is meaningful. One former executive sighed, "No matter what I do for the rest of my life, it won't matter as much as what I did when I was a CEO."

As you begin to slow down and pass the baton of leadership to your successor, you will need to face the challenge of finding meaning for the remaining years of your life.

Contribution

When asked the question, "What are you most proud of?" (aside from family), CEOs invariably respond with comments that relate to the positive contributions they have made in people's lives. They talk with pride about the great leaders who they have helped to develop, the wonderful jobs that they have helped to create, and the economic benefit that they have helped to generate.

Contribution and deeper meaning in life are often closely connected. Just as making a contribution contributes to pride and meaning, not making a contribution can lead to emptiness.

As you slow down and get ready to leave, you may need to find another way to make a contribution. If you think that you can just stop and watch the world go by, you may be disappointed.

The first step in letting go is to make an honest assessment of what you are letting go of. In walking away from the CEO role, you are letting go of a lot.

The vast majority of employees, who have never been in positions of true power, have no idea how difficult it can be to let go of authority. Most people believe, "With all of that money, I wouldn't have any trouble letting go of work. I would just have a great time hanging out at the beach for the rest of my life!" It is easy to imagine letting go of what you *never had*. It is hard to let go of what you *do have*.

I have seen too many CEOs deny their love for their jobs at the beginning of the succession process and then fail to pass the baton with dignity and class—as they calculate the cost of leaving—at the end of the succession process. Don't let this happen to you.

Moving On—Creating a Great "Rest of Your Life"

As you get ready to slow down and transition, you need to ask yourself an important question: "What am I going to do now?"

Frances Hesselbein is the former national executive director of the Girl Scouts of the USA and is now chairman of the Leader to Leader Institute. Peter Drucker considered Frances to be the greatest executive he had ever met. She is also a wonderful human being.

Alex von Bidder is co-owner of the Four Seasons in New York—one of the most famous and successful restaurants in the world. Alex is also a master yoga teacher and one of the deepest thinkers I've ever known.

On three different occasions (twice at my home in Rancho Santa Fe and once in New York), Frances, Alex, and I had the unique opportunity to spend a day and a half with three different sets of eight extremely accomplished people. The major topic of our open dialogue was "creating a great rest of my life."

The executives were at various stages of career and life. Like you, they were dealing with the process of letting go. Some had left their jobs two or three years earlier, some were just getting ready to depart, and some had a few years left before departure. Although they were from very different industries and backgrounds (some corporate, some nonprofit, and some military), they had a lot in common. And they were all there to learn from each other and to help each other.

You may benefit from spending time with a group like this as you prepare for your departure. The only people who can tell you "what it is really like" to live through CEO succession are the people who have done it!

Being the CEO of a publicly traded, multibillion-dollar corporation is a very unique experience. It is hard to really know what it is like, if you have not "lived there." That is why I think that it is a great idea for retiring CEOs to learn from other CEOs who have gone through the same transition.

In each session, participants' chairs were placed in a circle—with no furniture in the middle, no Power-Point presentations, no computers, and no notes. It was just human beings talking to each other for hours. The dialogue was amazingly open, candid, and supportive.

There's a lot of truth to the saying "It's lonely at the top." As you know, if you're the chief executive officer of a publicly traded, multibillion-dollar corporation, you can't stand up and share your "existential angst" with the world. You have to be "on" almost all of the time. This is an important part of being a professional and being a responsible leader.

But CEOs, like you, are just as human as the rest of us. They, too, have parents with Alzheimer's, spouses who get angry, kids with problems, and customers who can be very demanding. They have the same kinds of aspirations and concerns that come with growing older as all human beings.

During our time together, these leaders loved the opportunity to just be "people" and talk about their lives, their hopes, and their fears.

Looking from the outside in, we might logically assume that these people would be looking forward to retirement and a life of leisure. Wrong! None of these great leaders had the slightest desire to retire in the traditional sense.

In our discussions, the three most important variables that needed to be taken care of—in order to have a great "rest of my life"—were contribution, meaning, and happiness.

While some participants had more wealth than others, none believed money was a key factor in "creating a great rest of my life." Everyone agreed that while money can be used to pay for nice homes, fast cars, and fine dining, it can't be used to purchase meaning. Studies on happiness have also shown that, beyond a middle-income level, the amount of money one has bears almost no correlation to how happy one is. Although they missed the perks of being a CEO, most retirees realized that they could buy the really important benefits with the money that they had accumulated. The former CEOs who had dropped their competitive urge to make more money than their friends—or to make more money than they had made last year—were doing fine.

While everyone agreed that health was critically important, this group of twenty-four people was remarkably healthy. Health concerns were seldom discussed. In fact, several people commented on the fact that with good luck, a healthy lifestyle, and medical care, they might well be able to contribute to the world twenty or more years after leaving their "primary" occupation.

Everyone clearly valued relationships with friends and family members and saw that these relationships were a key factor in their future well-being. In spite of their amazingly busy schedules and demanding lives, these people had very positive, stable relationships with friends and family. Relationship concerns were not a major topic.

Although the CEOs who had left missed many of their colleagues, they still maintained close relationships with the ones who were personal friends.

Most of these executives spent their time discussing contribution, meaning, and happiness. In fact, these three themes were so closely intertwined that they were almost impossible to separate.

All of the participants at our sessions realized how blessed they were and wanted to give back in their later years, make a positive contribution to the world, and leave a legacy. They wanted to help others in the same way that mentors, teachers, parents, and friends had helped them.

Each person wanted to continue doing work that had true meaning. Instead of becoming a person who *used to be* making a difference, they all wanted to remain a person who *still was* making a difference. No one wanted to rest on their laurels while reviewing their scrapbooks and awards for the next twenty or thirty years.

Finally, all of the participants wanted to be happy. They realized that, at least for them, true happiness can't be bought—it has to be lived. They believed that, at a deeper level, happiness couldn't be separated from meaning and contribution, but could only come from meaning and contribution.

A lot has happened in the months that have passed since these meetings. One investment banker is now the CEO of one of the world's most important environmental organizations. He is dedicating his life to helping our planet. One executive is still leading, but is now leading a different major corporation, where she has even more opportunity to serve. Her challenges are huge, but she savors going to work every day. One adviser is still advising, but he's now advising people on how to have great lives, not just make more money. One started a new business, sold it, and is using her money to help mentor entrepreneurs. One of the most successful post-CEOs is focused on training the future executives in his region. He loves his work and is trying to give hundreds of younger leaders the wisdom that his mentors gave him.

I'm a very lucky person. Many years ago, one of my coaches, Richard Leider, taught me that reflecting on life and purpose is a process that should start when we're young—and never stop. I also had the privilege of serving on the board of the Peter F. Drucker Foundation for ten years and being able to observe Peter Drucker. Peter worked until his death at age ninety-six. He was never interested in retiring. He was never a "used to be." Through his wonderful example, I learned that making a difference means a lot more than making a living.

Think about the rest of your life. Now is a great time to start planning. Begin by challenging yourself. How can you make a contribution? How can you find meaning? What will really make you happy? You may well have twenty or thirty years to live after your present work is finished. How can you make this time count—for yourself and the people around you?

If you have options that you believe will lead to happiness, meaning, and contribution, you will be much more willing to let go when you should. If you look into the future and see nothing that looks exciting, you will be tempted to hang on longer than you should.

As you contemplate letting go of the baton of leadership, look for another track and another race. Planning for contribution, meaning, and happiness in your next life will not only help you, it will be good for your successor!

Your hand will be relaxed as you deal with succession and hand off the baton of leadership. You won't have white knuckles from holding on too tightly.

Finding Another Team—or Teams

My most common advice to CEOs who are dealing with succession in their sixties is to find another team—or sometimes, find some other teams. As we have discussed earlier, traditional retirement usually doesn't work. You will need to keep on contributing—just not with the same team.

As a CEO, you have become used to being surrounded by people who tell you how smart, creative, and wonderful you are. Don't get overly enamored with yourself when you start looking for the next challenge in life. Finding another great team might not be as easy as you think.

I was having dinner with one of the top officers in the U.S. Army. At the table were seven newly minted generals (all men). The senior officer laughed as he looked at their shiny new stars. As he contemplated finally leaving the military, he reflected back upon his own experience. He smiled as he joked around with the new generals: "Have you noticed that lately, whenever you tell a joke, everyone laughs? You aren't that funny! Have you noticed that lately, whenever you make a comment, people nod in agreement? You aren't that smart! Have you noticed that lately, women seem to want to have sex with you? You aren't that handsome!" He grew serious, sighed, and continued, "Always remember, they are not saluting *you*. They are saluting that star on your shoulder—all that it stands for—and all that it has stood for over the years. Never let admiration go to your head. When you quit wearing that star, they won't be saluting anymore."

As soon as you stop being a CEO, you will learn that the old officer was right—not just about them, but about you. When you are a CEO they are not "saluting" you because you are funny, smart, and handsome. They are saluting you because you are the CEO. When you leave your position, this will become painfully obvious—very quickly.

As we have discussed, in looking at the rest of your life, you will need to find something to do that provides happiness, meaning, and contribution. From my observation, this might not be as easy as you think it will be.

Your first challenge may be getting over your own ego and sense of importance.

One of my favorite coaching clients is the CEO of a huge company. He is going to be leaving in about six months—and has done absolutely nothing to plan for his departure. I asked him, "If you knew that your company was going to face a major, dramatic change in six months, would you start developing a strategy to deal with this change now?"

"Of course," he replied.

I replied, "Your entire life is going to face a major, dramatic change in six months. You may not realize this right now, but ultimately, your life is even more important than this company. Start developing a strategy for the rest of your life!"

You should talk with this CEO! Perhaps you two could help each other.

When you are looking for a future position (or a combination of interesting activities), I have one consistent suggestion. Get real offers! Don't worry too much about money, perks, status, or power. Focus on a position that will lead to happiness, meaning, and contribution. Get real offers—then weigh the costs and benefits—and make real decisions.

My friend Randy is an excellent example. Randy had a fantastic career in a top professional services company. In spite of his outstanding contribution to the business, he was in his early sixties, and according to this company's published guidelines, it was time to go. He was very dynamic and had no interest in traditional retirement. He knew that he wanted an exciting new career challenge for the next few years, but wasn't sure what. We discussed his future, and he started thinking about leadership in the nonprofit sector.

"Perhaps I should be a leader in a human services firm," he mused enthusiastically. "I really don't need much money, and this would give me an opportunity to make a positive contribution to society. I believe that a lot of what I have learned in business could be applied in the social sector. And who knows? At my age, this type of change might be great fun for me."

His face changed expression as he began to debate with himself. "On the other hand, I'm not sure that

I want to spend all of my time taking rich old people out for lunch and begging them for money," he fretted. "That may be a large part of my job as a nonprofit leader. And sometimes those nonprofit people look down on businesspeople like me. They think we are all just greedy capitalists with no real values."

Randy had similar debates with himself about consulting, private equity, and a couple of other future careers. As he began his search for a new job, he didn't do very well. Some potential organizations saw him as arrogant. They felt he showed more interest in "What can you do for me?" or "Would you like to know how wonderful I am?" than "What can I do for you?" He asked a lot of questions he could have answered himself had he done more homework; they felt he communicated with ambiguity and showed a lack of genuine desire for the new job.

Randy became a little defensive as he and I discussed some of the negative feedback from the companies where he had interviewed. "I am not really sure what I want," he snapped. "What's wrong with me asking a few questions? And by the way, I'm not so sure I would have wanted those jobs anyway!"

I gave Randy the career advice I give most often: get real offers. "Why don't you go out, do your homework, sell yourself better, and get some specific offers in writing?" I asked. "Until you get real offers, most of your internal debating is just hypothetical, a waste of time. From what I have heard from you so far, I think that there are some positions in the non-profit world that you would love—and others that you couldn't stand. My guess is that the same thing is true for private equity or consulting. Get real offers—with real salaries, real job descriptions, real cowork-ers, and real board members. Then you can do apples-to-apples comparisons and figure out which position you like the best. It doesn't really matter how you feel about a job you will never get anyway."

Randy changed his attitude, did his homework, and started going for real offers. He dropped his "Are you good enough for me?" questioning and started selling himself and his potential to make a contribution. He quit doing informational interviews that made it seem as if he were judging the organization's worth, and focused on organizations that might be a fit.

Within a few months, he had some real alterna-tives. Although there was much he liked about the nonprofit world, he realized that his options there were not nearly as exciting (to him) as leadership in a venture capital (VC) firm. He decided that he could help society more by making money and giving it to other nonprofit leaders who would be better at human services management than he was. He deeply respected the specific board members and coworkers in his new VC firm and decided that he was going to have a lot of fun as a venture capitalist.

My advice for you, if you're facing transition and are getting stuck in a mental debate among competing potential career options is, focus your energy on getting offers. When you get real offers, you can make real decisions. At the end of the day, all job offers are good. And even if you say no to an offer, you will probably have learned something in the process—even if it's learning what you don't want. And it's nice to be asked.

Although some career counselors may disagree with my advice, I generally think it is better to start the process of getting real offers *before* you leave your present role.

You may not want to get one offer, but instead work on several smaller projects. One of the happiest and fulfilled retired executives I know, is on several boards, spends more (but not too much) time with her family, and works on three different charitable causes.

As you begin the handoff process, you will need to let go of leading the company and focus on developing your successor. As the handoff time nears, you will need to let go of developing your successor and focus on creating a great rest of your life.

PART II

Choosing Your Successor

3 Choosing Who to Develop as Your Successor

The development of a great successor is one of the most important accomplishments that a CEO can achieve. But should you develop an internal or an external successor?

The Case for Internal Successors

There are many reasons, both personal and professional, to make the investment in developing your successor from candidates *inside* the company.

The Costs of External CEO Failure

To begin with, if you hire a CEO from outside the company, the board will expect a "name brand" leader who has a proven track record of success. There aren't that many out there! To hire such an executive, you are going to have to pay a ton of money and provide an expensive golden parachute if things don't work out. Several recent disaster stories (Home Depot, Hewlett-Packard, etc.) have shown exactly how much this type of failure can cost the company. The main damage to the company, however, is not the actual amount of money spent; it is the damage to the corporate reputation. CEOs from the outside who fail—and then get tens or even hundreds of millions of dollars from the company for getting fired—provide incredibly negative stories for the business press that can lead to long-term PR damage for the corporation.

While the damage done by a failed external CEO is bad outside the company, it is even worse *inside* the company. When chief executives fail, employees are often dismissed and resources are cut. It is very hard to explain to twenty-year veteran employees why they have to take less so a failed externally hired CEO can get more.

In short, hiring a name brand CEO from outside the company who fails is usually a disaster. The board of directors looks like a group of idiots who have only succeeded in embarrassing the company and wasting money. This sad drama only reinforces the increasingly common perception that CEOs are overpaid and that executives and board members are ultimately looking out for their own interests—not the interests of the company.

Since you are the former CEO, who is part of the selection process, your own reputation is going to go down with that of the company. This is certainly not the legacy that you want to leave.

There is no research that shows external CEOs to be superior to internal CEOs in producing long-term returns to the corporation. While they may bring the advantage of an external perspective, they come with the disadvantage of not knowing the internal workings of the company and, in some cases, not even knowing the industry.

One former CEO, after listening to my discussion on this topic, pointed out that while the CEO may support the internal successor, the board may become enamored with the "glamour" of a proven external candidate. He noted that one challenge of the CEO could be managing the egos of board members who may find the internal candidate less personally exciting and who like to hang out with other famous leaders from the outside.

I am not suggesting that companies should always hire internal candidates. There are obviously case studies where external CEOs have made a huge positive difference (e.g., IBM). I am suggesting that external CEOs come with extremely high risk and that you should develop an internal successor if at all possible.

The Wrong Message About Leadership Development

I teach in a corporate leadership development program with one very famous CEO who was hired from outside the company. This executive personally instructs management training courses for vice presidents and above. In each session, he makes the point that his own hiring is indicative of a failure in leadership development for the company. He clearly states his personal commitment to nurture talent from within—and to develop his own successor.

Your company is asking leaders at all levels to develop talent. Every manager has to answer the question "If you were hit by a bus tomorrow, who could take your place?" What message is sent to your leaders when you, as a CEO, cannot develop your own successor? This indicates that you have not been practicing what you preach in terms of development. Do you want to send a message to employees that you have not succeeded in doing something that you have been asking frontline supervisors to do for years?

As of this writing, recent meltdowns in the financial markets exposed how clearly unprepared several of the world's leading banks were for CEO succession.

To make it worse, external CEOs often bring trusted high-level executives from their former

44

companies with them. This means that internal executives are dismissed and that promotion opportunities are removed. Leaders at many levels can begin to feel like failures. These personnel changes may well result in valued employees leaving the corporation, since they fear that they probably won't be in line for future promotions—and may well get fired. Is this what you want to happen to the people who have supported you for all of these years?

The Positive Impact of Internal Succession

While hiring a CEO from the outside brings great risk and sends the wrong message about development, effective internal succession can produce the opposite, positive outcomes.

Hiring a candidate from the inside shows that you, as a CEO, have made the same effort to develop internal talent that you are asking of everyone else. As your successor moves up to the CEO role, a top-level position opens up so that another internal executive can be promoted.

You have a vision for the company. After putting in years to make this vision a reality, you find it important that your vision continue after you leave the company. By developing an internal successor, you can be more assured that your vision will be carried out after you depart. While you want your successor to bring a fresh perspective, you don't want her to negate all that you have done in the past.

By carefully developing your successor from inside the company, you can dramatically increase the probability of a positive transition and a successful future.

In developing your successor, remember that the CEO transition process is extremely personal. While my prior notes have been aimed at helping you face the reality of passing the baton of leadership—and getting *you* ready for the handoff—future sections will be aimed at helping you get your *successor* ready to take the baton and ultimately become a great leader for your company.

How the Business Environment Can Eliminate an Internal Successor

While the development of an internal successor may be your goal, there are sometimes forces in the business environment that eliminate this possibility.

In one famous case, a major corporate ethics violation led to the selection of an external, rather than internal, CEO. One high-level executive committed an ethics violation that embarrassed the company's major client. While the CEO was not directly involved in the violation, he was held responsible for the ensuing damage that followed. Although the company had a very well-qualified internal candidate, an outsider was chosen. This was seen as sending the right message from the board about the severity of the problems and the company's need to change.

In another case, the company's market was rapidly changing. It's bread-and-butter product was becoming obsolete. The board needed to send a message to investors and customers that the company was headed in an entirely different direction. The new CEO came in with credibility in a field that no one in the company could match.

In a third case, the internal candidate was seen as being a *potentially* excellent CEO, but a series of events led to the hiring of an outsider who was seen as an even better CEO *immediately*. The company's challenges were so severe that the board did not feel it had the luxury of waiting for a great leader to develop.

When should you *not* develop your successor from inside the company? While the answer is complex at one level, it is simple at another level. Do a cost-benefit analysis. What are the costs of bringing in an outsider? What are the potential benefits? What are the costs of promoting each specific candidate? What are the potential benefits?

Finally, are there any available outsiders who are so gifted that no one in the company can match their potential contribution? If the answer is a clear "yes," hire them. If the answer is "not sure" or "no," promote an insider.

4 Evaluating Internal Coaching Candidates

Along with being your company's CEO, you may get to have another great job. You may get to be the *coach* for your company's next CEO! Even if you hire an external coach to help out, you can and should be involved and help ensure the success of the coaching process.

Being a CEO Coach

I have spent more than thirty years coaching executives—and I love it! There is no reason that you shouldn't enjoy your role as the coach for a future CEO as much as I do. Given your experience as a CEO and your unique perspective on the company, I also believe that, in many ways, you can be an even more effective coach for your successor than I can.

Let me share the highlights of what I have learned about behavioral coaching with you—and then talk about how you can apply my coaching process in coaching your successor.

In my work as a coach, I don't get paid if my clients don't achieve positive, lasting change in behavior. This positive change is not determined by me or my clients; it is determined by the key stakeholders that surround my clients. Although I usually get paid, I sometimes fail. I will share what I have learned from both my successes and my failures: *a wise person learns from their mistakes—a much wiser person learns from someone else's mistakes*.

My suggestions will *only* focus on helping your successor achieve positive change in *behavior*. I can't help you with strategic, technical, or functional coaching. In any case, at the potential CEO level, the huge majority of requests for coaching are behavioral. Candidates who lack strategic, technical, or functional skills are generally out of the running before immediate CEO succession is even discussed.

In almost every case, there are certain behaviors that, if your successor changes, will positively impact his chance of becoming a great CEO. If your successor is human, he is being considered for this job *because of* doing many things right. He is probably also being considered for the role *in spite of* some behaviors that need to change. My next few sections will give you a plan for dealing with these in-spite-of behaviors.

I will also discuss the relationship of your successor with key stakeholders. As we discussed earlier, CEO transition is a very personal process. It is not just personal for you and your successor; it is also personal for her key stakeholders. As a coach, your goal should be to make her as effective as possible in dealing with them—and them as effective as possible in dealing with her.

Your time is valuable, and the succession decision is critical for you and your company. Let's begin with three qualifying questions to determine if behavioral coaching may be useful in the development of your successor.

Do *You* Really Want Him to Be the Next CEO?

I learned a great lesson on a CEO succession-coaching assignment where I *did* get paid—but ended up wishing that I *hadn't* taken the job.

A major CEO asked me to coach his CFO—and potential successor. After a few minutes I had the distinct feeling that the CEO just didn't *like* the CFO— and didn't really want him to get the job.

"I don't think that you *like* this guy," I said to the CEO.

"He may not be my favorite person, but I guess that I like him OK." The CEO's reply didn't come with a great deal of conviction.

"Look, it's just you and me talking here. There is no reason to play games with me," I challenged. "I don't think you like the CFO. If you really don't want him to get this job, why are we even having this conversation? I don't even know this guy. I don't care if he becomes the CEO or not. Why would you want me to coach him—or to work on developing him as your successor—if you really don't want him to have the job?"

"You are right!" he grunted. "I don't like this guy. I think that he is kind of a jerk. I have never liked him very much—even though I've tried."

"Then why are we having this conversation?" I asked.

He replied, "I don't like him much, but I have to admit, he has made a tremendous contribution in helping our company. We have done a fantastic turnaround—and without him it would have been impossible. If your coaching process can really help him improve his interpersonal skills, he deserves to be the CEO of the company."

"Are you sure?" I enquired skeptically.

"I think so—no, I am positive," he replied.

When I heard, "I think so," my gut said, "Leave now!" Unfortunately, I didn't.

"If he makes great improvement in the interpersonal areas that we discussed, are you going to recommend him to be your successor?" I asked. "Are there *any* other reasons he may not get the job, such as a lack of technical or functional skills?"

"No, along with being great in finance, he is strong enough in all of the other functions to do a fine job as the chief executive," the CEO concluded. "His only issues revolve around interpersonal behavior."

I worked with the CFO for more than a year. At the end of my assignment, he was seen as making great improvements in all his targeted areas for interpersonal change—by fifteen out of sixteen raters. Only one person saw "no change." Guess who that was? The CEO.

After the CFO confronted the CEO with his obvious improvement in interpersonal relationships, the CEO still did not recommend him for the job. While the CEO reluctantly admitted that the CFO had made great improvement in interpersonal behavior—which was clearly documented and hard to dispute—he now concluded that the CFO lacked "adequate marketing skills." This was the same CEO who had told me the CFO's marketing skills were just fine one year earlier.

Needless to say, the CFO was incensed. He pointed out that he had been assured that he would get the "big job" if he improved his interpersonal skills. He mentioned that he had turned down other, lucrative offers since he had assumed he would get the CEO position. He went to the board, pointed out what happened, and basically said, "Either make me the new CEO—or write me an extremely large check."

He was paid off by the board—which cost the company millions of dollars. Since he had clearly improved, I was paid for my work as his coach. I still wished that I hadn't taken the assignment. In hindsight, I feel that I was used as a pawn in a political game. The CEO believed that the CFO would not improve, and then he could say, "Well, we tried to help him. We got him the best coach we could find. He still didn't improve; therefore, he is not ready for the job."

When the CFO did improve, the CEO had to play the embarrassing "lacks marketing skills" card. My work—and the CFO's great effort—ended up costing the company lots of money. At least the CFO was grateful to me—and felt he could use what he had learned in our work together in future roles.

Since that event, I have had other experiences that have reinforced my belief that if you, as the CEO, really don't want a potential successor to get the job, you aren't going to be helpful in coaching.

What is the learning point from this story for you, as a CEO? Look in the mirror. If you really don't want your potential successor to get the job, don't kid yourself. There is a very strong probability that this person will never get the job. You will just look for problems until you find a reason to disqualify him.

Don't jerk around potential successors. This is not fair to them or to the company. If, in your heart, you don't want the person to be your successor, don't pretend to be interested in developing him for the job. Just work with someone you can support. If you cannot find a successor who you can sincerely support, go to the outside immediately and start recruiting some new talent!

Will She Be Given a Fair Chance by Her Key *Stakeholders*?

You may personally believe that a potential successor is perfect for the job, and you may do a great job in coaching her so that she is ready for the job, but if the board decides not to hire her, it won't matter. When you are coaching your potential successor, it is critical that she establish positive board relationships before the succession decision is made.

One of my potential CEO clients lost it in one meeting with the board, got angry, tried to prove a board member was wrong, and succeeded in alienating several important people on the board. This type of damage is hard to repair. A year later, when I interviewed board members about this candidate, a couple of board members brought up this event. Even though the candidate's behavior had been stellar for the past year, the event was stuck in their minds and was seen as symbolic of the negative behavior of this executive.

It is important for you, as a coach, to thoroughly prepare your successor for board meetings. It can be useful to have detailed discussions about the preferences, views, and quirks of each board member.

In other cases, a potential successor may have fine relationships with the board, but be sabotaged by peers. In one of my "failure" coaching experiences, I tried to explain to peers how my job was to help a candidate achieve positive, lasting change in behavior—not only to improve his effectiveness in his current position, but to help him prepare for a potential promotion. It was clear that the peer group basically hated this person and had no desire to help him get promoted. In fact, a few made it clear that they would be much happier if they could help him get fired!

This person was eventually removed from serious consideration for the role of CEO. It became clear to the existing CEO and the board that he had been written off by many important peers and was never going to be given a fair opportunity by them—no matter what he did or how hard he tried.

My final example of a stakeholder veto comes from a chief executive of the company's leading customer. In this case, the CEO of the customer's organization felt that, years before, he had been insulted by the potential successor, who was, at the time, in a sales role. Although this event had happened years before, the customer CEO had never forgiven this candidate and still considered him to be a total jerk. The customer CEO also happened to be friends with a couple of members of the board. Although this candidate may well have been qualified for the job— and had the support of his CEO and peers—he was not even considered for the position. Big customers count!

Before spending your time developing your successor, make a critical stakeholder assessment. Ask an important question: "Will this candidate be given a fair chance, not only by me, but also by the key stakeholders who are critical to her future success?"

If this answer is no—and if you cannot change key stakeholder perceptions—look for another candidate. When critical stakeholders have written off candidates, their succession possibilities may be over—no matter what you, or they, do to change behavior.

If it eventually becomes obvious that board members or other key stakeholders have vetoed your favorite candidate—and that she is not going to get the job—your path is simple—start over! You, as the CEO, will need to let go of your disappointment and do your best to support another potential candidate who can be approved by the board.

Is *He* Willing to Make an Authentic Effort to Change?

The hardest lesson that I have learned as a coach is that none of my clients are going to get better because of *me*. My efforts to "save" people who had no interest in changing have all been a complete waste of time. I hate to tell you this, but—as hard as it may be for you, as the CEO, to hear it—your successor is not going to achieve positive, lasting change because *you* are a great coach. If he is going to achieve positive change, the deep motivation for this change will have to come from inside *him*.

(As an aside, this learning is not only important at work. It is even important at home. Have you ever attempted to change the behavior of a spouse, partner, parent, or significant other who had no interest in changing? How well did that work for you? One of the classic problems of retired chief executives is that they become bored and engage in misguided efforts to "manage" or "coach" their friends and family members! Let me help you. This is a disaster!)

After performing a careful analysis of existing and desired leadership behavior, you and he will need to determine what changes are needed to help him take it to the next level, become a great CEO, and have effective relationships with his key stakeholders.

One of the greatest frustrations that I hear from CEOs in describing potential successors is, "If he only made this one change, he could become so much more effective. *I have told him this over and over.* Why doesn't *he* just do it?"

As Arnold Schwarzenegger so wisely noted, "Nobody ever got muscles by watching me lift weights."

You can *help* your successor achieve authentic change. You cannot *make* your successor achieve authentic change.

Assuming that your successor can benefit from changing behavior, you will first need to decide if this behavioral change is a "game-breaker." In other words, if the change does occur, he should be your successor; if it doesn't, he shouldn't. You will then need to make a judgment call.

Does he *really* want to change because he believes that this is the right thing to do for both him and the company—or is he only going through the motions because he wants to be the next CEO?

In my own coaching with potential chief executives, I am clear that I only want to work with them if they believe changed leadership behavior is the right thing to do for them, their team members, and their companies. If I believe that they are only interested in changing to get ahead, I refuse to work with them.

If you believe that the change is vitally important, and you believe that your successor is only going through the motions—as painful as it may be—find another successor. If he is just faking it to *become* a CEO, what will happen when he gets promoted and *is* the CEO? His dysfunctional behavior will not only return—it may become even worse.

If he needs to achieve positive change in behavior, and if he is sincerely willing to try, you can definitely help him get better—*if* he will be given a fair chance not only by you, but by other key stakeholders.

PART III

Coaching Your Successor

5   Beginning the Coaching Process

Should you hire an external executive coach? Since I provide executive coaching for a living, it is a little hard for me to be objective in answering this question. Let me give you my guidelines on when, how, and if you should hire an executive coach.

Deciding on an Executive Coach

To begin with, make a rough analysis of the needs of the potential CEO. This memo focuses on *behavioral* coaching—because that is all that I know. What if your successor needs help in a different area?

In hiring an executive coach, do *not* describe the needs of your successor and then ask the coach if she is qualified to handle this type of challenge. Begin by asking the coach to describe her area of specialty. For example, my own area of expertise involves helping successful leaders achieve positive, lasting change in leadership behavior. I don't do strategic, functional, technical, how-to-give-speeches, or how-to-get-organized coaching. There is absolutely nothing wrong with these types of coaching. They are just not what I do.

I get ridiculous requests for coaching. One pharmaceutical company wanted me to coach a potential head of R&D. When I asked about the major challenge faced by the person, I was told, "He is not updated on medical technology!" I replied, "Neither am I!" I cannot help a bad scientist become a good scientist or a bad engineer become a good engineer. If your potential successor needs to brush up on skills in marketing or finance, he needs to find a coach who has expertise in providing advice in that field. There are very few strategists in the world who I would recommend. Great thinkers like C. K. Prahalad or Vijay Govindarajan could help far more than I could. Your successor's strategic vision may well determine the future of the company. Be very careful about who you ask for advice in this area. Far too many "experts" pretend to be knowledgeable about strategic coaching, when their backgrounds show that they are not at all qualified to give advice on strategy. While I am not an expert on strategy, at least I know enough to know that I am not an expert. I have met "strategy coaches" who know even less than me, yet pass themselves off as advisers in strategy.

If your successor needs coaching in a specific area, hire a coach who specializes in that field. For example, David Allen is a true expert on personal productivity and getting organized. Andrew Sobel and David Maister are experts in professional services. Robert Dilenschneider is an expert on executive presence.

At the CEO level, most requests for coaching are behavioral—not technical, functional, or strategic.

What are the advantages of an external executive behavioral coach?

The first advantage of an outside coach is confidentiality in collecting data. It can be hard for insiders to get valid information about a potential chief executive. Outsiders tend to be more trusted for this type of data collection.

A second advantage of an outside coach is credibility. If your successor needs help in a certain area, you may have high credibility as a CEO, yet have low credibility as a coach or teacher.

A third advantage of an outside coach is time. I have never met a CEO who wasn't extremely busy. How much time are you willing to devote to the coaching process?

When I was asked by one CEO, who I knew very well, to coach a potential successor, I asked, "Why do you want me to do this? You have been to my classes several times. You understand my coaching process as well as I do. Why don't you just do it yourself?"

He laughed and replied, "To begin with, you love this type of work more than I do, so you have more *motivation* than me. Second, although you say I can do this as well as you, I think that you have more *ability* as a coach than I do. Third, I am totally overcommitted and don't have the *time* to do this on my own. Fourth, your fees are high, but you make a lot less than I do. So hiring you will save the company a lot of *money*."

Although I ended up coaching his successor, the CEO remained involved in the process and was a key player in its success.

In most cases I believe that hiring an executive coach can be a useful part of the succession process. You, as the CEO, need to take responsibility for the entire process. You know a whole lot more about what it takes to be the next leader of your company than any outsider does.

In my upcoming notes, I will share my coaching process with you. You can review my ideas, do what you think works for you, and then hire an outsider to do whatever you feel can be best outsourced to an executive coach.

Every Meeting for the Rest of My Career?

Assuming that your successor has at least some work to do in improving stakeholder relationships, that she is motivated to change, and that she will be given a fair chance, it is now time to get started in your role as her coach.

Mary is one of the greatest CEOs who I have ever met. I think that you might be able to learn something from her interaction with Rob, her potential successor.

"Does this mean that I have to watch what I say—and worry about how I act—in *every* meeting for the *rest of my career?*" Rob, the potential CEO, grumbled.

I had been asked by Mary to coach Rob, who was then a division president. As part of our coaching process, Rob was asked to seek feedback from all of his key stakeholders—including Mary.

Mary was giving Rob feedback on his recent behavior in a team meeting—behavior that was viewed by some colleagues as inappropriate for a division president. Overall, Rob was seen as a strategic genius, with an amazing business mind, who was also rough around the edges in his dealings with people. He was viewed as sometimes making off-the-cuff comments that could be very hurtful to others. Rob's reaction to this feedback indicated that he believed some of the stakeholder comments were a little picky—and that some of his colleagues were being unduly critical.

"Welcome to my world!" Mary sighed. "If you ever want to become a CEO, get used to it. People are going to be listening to what you say—and watching how you act—in every meeting for the rest of your career. You should be thankful that you are getting this honest feedback—and that you are being given the opportunity to learn from it!"

Mary's advice was so true. As you know better than I, the higher up you go in an organization, the more people will be listening to your every word—and interpreting your every action.

As the world has changed, the role of the CEO has changed. The good news for chief executives is that you make lots more money. The bad news is that you are under far more scrutiny—and face much more pressure than ever before. In the old days, the business press was much more likely to give big executives like you a pass on modest displays of inappropriate behavior. Those days are over. With the advent of the Internet, the slightest faux pas can be recorded—or even videoed by an unseen cell phone—and sent to thousands of people around the world in minutes.

As an example, consider the way the White House press treated presidents before Richard Nixon, as opposed to the way that they have treated modern presidents, such as Bill Clinton and George W. Bush. A president's personal behavior is no longer considered off limits. It is now constantly being viewed under a microscope, with hopes of finding any blemish. Even normal human reactions in meetings, such as yawning, can be photographed and become fodder for late-night comedians.

Although the press has become increasingly critical, the most important reason for your successor to worry about the impact of her behavior is not the media; it is the potential impact of her behavior on the people she is leading.

As a leader, your successor needs to clearly understand—before taking the job—how much *CEO behavior matters* to the people she will be leading. If she wants to be a great leader, she will need to "make peace" with watching what she says and observing how she acts—for the rest of her career.

As you have learned, some parts of being a CEO are very exhilarating, like rallying the troops, achieving the vision, or celebrating great success; others can be excruciatingly dull, yet still very important. No one ever made a movie about leaders who were sitting through long meetings or watching slide shows; but as you know, that is a lot of what you, as the CEO and representative of the company, have been doing—every day, over and over.

Let's face it: your successor, like you, will spend hour after hour listening to potentially boring Power-Point presentations—on topics that he has already been briefed on. He needs to realize that these presentations may be the summary result of months of effort by employees at all levels in your organization. He needs to understand how much these employees care about their CEO's reaction. He will need to actively listen—and communicate with caring, interest, and enthusiasm—no matter how tired he may feel on the inside. He needs to realize that everyone will not only be listening to his words—everyone will be watching his face. Signs of boredom or indifference that may be ignored if coming from peers can be demoralizing when coming from CEOs. Signs of recognition and support can validate employees and provide needed recognition and inspiration after a great effort.

One great CEO coaching example (in New York) involved a comparison with actors on Broadway. Bill, the CEO, was coaching John, his successor.

"Have you ever been to a Broadway play?" Bill asked John.

"Of course," John replied, "but what does that have to do with becoming a great CEO?"

"While they were up on stage, did any of the actors ever complain because they had a headache, their aunt died, or the room was too hot?" Coach Bill continued.

"Of course not," Successor John replied, "the actor would be fired immediately if he ever did something that stupid."

"One thing I love about Broadway plays is that whenever the actors go out on the stage, it is *showtime*. These people put whatever worries they have behind them and put their soul into the job. They do this not because they are phonies; they do this because they are professionals. When you become a CEO, remember the actors on Broadway. You are making a lot more money than they are. If they can go out there every night, no matter how many times they have done it before, and give it their best—so can you. If you don't want to exhibit this kind of dedication—this level of professionalism—you shouldn't take the job and you don't deserve the money. Every day, when you have to make a presentation in front of key stakeholders, you are going to be the face of our company. Always remember, no matter how tired you may be, lots of people are looking at your face and counting on you. It is showtime!"

If your successor truly wants to become a great CEO, she needs to recognize that there is no "off" switch when she is around the people who she will be leading. From day one, she needs to understand that her increased authority will come with both increased scrutiny and increased responsibility.

The next time she is in a meeting with you and the executive team and she starts to become bored or tunes out, have her imagine that she is on video. Have her imagine that her words, actions, and even expressions are being taped and sent to people who care.

When she is a CEO, she will need to continuously look at the faces of the people she is leading—she won't need to imagine then. They *will* be listening; they *will* be watching; and they *will* care.

Your successor's behavior will matter—a lot—and she needs to learn how to act like a CEO *before* she gets the job, not after.

Involving Key Stakeholders in Determining Strengths and Challenges

After you hand off the baton of leadership to your successor, most of the key stakeholders involved in the coaching process will remain with the company. As we discussed earlier, key stakeholders can sometimes veto a candidate and eliminate the possibility of promotion. Even if they cannot cast a veto, it is important to involve key stakeholders in the development of your successor for a variety of reasons:

- After becoming the CEO, she will need the support of key stakeholders to turn *succession*

into *success*. No leader can do it alone. Your
successor will need lots of help to make a
graceful transition—especially early in her role
as CEO. Working to improve relationships
before the transition can pay great dividends
after the transition.

- If your efforts at coaching are strictly based
  upon *your* perceptions, you may be completely
  missing the perceptions of important
  stakeholders—who may be hesitant to point
  out that you, the CEO, are wrong.

- You aren't that smart! Your successor will learn
  a lot more when he gets input from you *and* his
  key stakeholders—not just you. You can be more
  effective by becoming a coach who facilitates
  learning from multiple sources rather than a
  coach who plays the role of CEO know-it-all.

- Stakeholders who are trying to help your
  successor improve become psychologically
  invested in helping her "win," as opposed to
  letting her "lose." Remember, it is just as
  important to help stakeholders build effective
  relationships with your successor as it is to help
  your successor build effective relationships
  with them.

- The effectiveness of your successor's behavior cannot be judged in a vacuum. It can only be determined by the key stakeholders who are impacted by this behavior. Positive indications of change from many important people are much more valid than positive indications of change from one person—even if that person is you.

You can encourage key stakeholders to help your successor by asking each of them to:

- *Be open minded—and not stereotype your potential successor.* We all tend to see behavior in others that is consistent with our previous stereotype. For example, if stakeholders believe that your successor is a bad listener, they will look for a bad listener in interpersonal interactions. If they are open minded to the entire spectrum of his behavior, they will see both positive and negative examples of listening. By being open minded, they can focus on helping him get better, as opposed to proving they were right—about his behavior that needs to change.

- *Focus on the future—not the past.* Stakeholders should focus on the future in two ways:

(1) place more effort in providing ideas on what can be changed tomorrow—not reciting what went wrong yesterday and (2) give suggestions aimed at helping the successor become a great CEO—not just becoming more effective in her present position. Encourage them to focus on a future that can be changed—not a past that cannot be changed.

- *Be helpful and supportive—not cynical, sarcastic, or judgmental.* If key stakeholders work to help your successor in a positive way, your successor will probably respond in a positive way. If they act in a negative way, your successor will just tune out and quit listening to their advice. No one likes pain. If the coaching process becomes painful, your successor will be more focused on avoidance than positive change.

- *Tell the truth—and avoid sugarcoating reality.* Your successor is not going to benefit from false praise. While honest feedback can be painful before he gets the job, the costs of mistakes will be much higher after he gets the job. This type of honesty requires courage from stakeholders—who may be afraid of repercussions after your successor is promoted.

- *Pick a behavior of their own to improve—not just work to improve your successor*. Your successor is much more likely to see the change process in a positive light if *everyone* is trying to improve—rather than just putting her in the spotlight. This makes the entire process two-way instead of one-way. It helps the stakeholders act as "fellow travelers" who are trying to improve, not "judges" who are pointing their fingers at your successor. It also greatly expands the value gained by the corporation in your coaching process. For example, in the case of one of my favorite clients, I was asked by the CEO to coach one person: his potential successor. At the end of the coaching process, more than one hundred stakeholders were documented as having achieved positive change. Why? His stakeholders were all focused on improving themselves—as well as helping him get better.

While no individual stakeholder comments should be public information, the fact that your successor is working on personal improvement—and the areas that he is working on—should be openly discussed. Our research on stakeholder involvement is clear. When stakeholders do not know what the leader is trying to improve and when open discussions on improvement are not held, there is far less chance that the successor will achieve positive change over time.

I am a believer in measurement. If the potential CEO's areas for improvement are not openly discussed with key stakeholders, how can positive change (as judged by key stakeholders) ever be measured? If there is no measurement, how can the success of any change initiative ever be known?

Which Key Stakeholders Should Be Involved?

As we discussed, when you are preparing your successor for the personal side of CEO transition, she will need to get different types of feedback that represent different—yet equally important—stakeholder perspectives.

Board members can describe their perceptions on how your successor comes across in board meetings. In many cases they will also have informal feedback about how your successor deals with peers and direct reports. In many cases board members do not have extensive personal experience in working with the potential CEO. Their perceptions may have been formed on the basis of isolated events or secondhand reports. This doesn't matter. Board members are still board members. They are important stakeholders, and your successor needs to know their *perceptions* concerning her behavior.

Peers can describe how your successor succeeds or fails in developing collaborative, win-win relationships with them. Peer feedback is very important because these stakeholders are currently members of *your* management team—and will soon become members of *his* management team. When your successor is getting feedback from peers, it is important to be sensitive to political motivations. In most cases, at least some of the peers will believe that *they* are more qualified than the person you want to be your successor. They may not feel very motivated to make your successor look good when they provide feedback.

Direct reports can share information on how your successor comes across in a leadership role. They can describe what it is like to have this person as their "boss." As a CEO, you need to be sensitive to the fact that some leaders are very skilled at coming across one way to the people above them in the organization— and a very different way to the employees below them in the organization. When he is a CEO, everyone in the company will report to him.

In some cases, *customer* or *supplier* feedback may also be very useful. If the company is primarily serving many transactional customers who have no direct contact with executives, then customer feedback may not be valid. If the company is primarily serving a smaller number of key relationship customers who do have meaningful contact with executives, customer feedback can be critically important. Similar reservations and benefits would apply to transactional or relationship suppliers.

Ask this question: "What key stakeholder relationships are most critical for me, as a CEO, to ensure that I do a great job in leading our company?" Make a list of names. All of these names should be on the "feedback list" for your successor.

When data is being gathered from key stakeholders, it is important to recognize that some might be biased, some might be acting on incomplete data, and some might just have differing opinions. Look for clear patterns in the data. If one or two stakeholders have an issue, it may be their problem, not your successor's. If many have the same issue, it is probably your successor's problem!

If your successor doesn't know some of these people, she should get to know them before the transition occurs.

6 Becoming a CEO Coach-Facilitator

When you are collecting feedback from key stake-holders, there is no need to reinvent the wheel. Any executive who has reached the level of serious CEO consideration has probably received several different forms of feedback in the past. As we discussed earlier, this memo will focus on *behavioral* coaching. It is assumed that the candidate has the strategic skills, functional talent, and track record of results needed to qualify for the job.

Reviewing Previous Feedback

Many large organizations make regular use of *360°
feedback*. This type of feedback is generally presented as a summary of numerical ratings and written com-ments that have been collected from direct reports and other coworkers. In most cases the respondents are not individually identified, so the feedback tends

to be more honest than that provided in public. When you are analyzing 360° reports, it is important to:

- *Look for trends.* If scores on selected areas for improvement show progress over time, the candidate may well be a person who responds well to input—and works to get better. If the scores never improve, the candidate may be a person who has not made a significant effort to improve in the past.

- *Consider environmental factors.* If the candidate has been asked to turn around a difficult organization, he may have had to make decisions that were not pleasing to the employees—but correct for the company. Leadership is not a popularity contest. I used to be a dean. In reviewing research on teacher feedback from students, I learned that there was a clear correlation between the grades that students gave the teachers—and the grades that teachers gave the students. Sometimes this candidate may have given tough performance reviews or even dismissed key employees. In these cases, 360° feedback scores may well suffer.

- *Find key patterns.* I have reviewed thousands of 360° feedback summaries. There are almost

always clear patterns in both the areas of
strength and in the areas for improvement.
Look for the few key areas for development
that you believe will make the most difference
in helping this candidate become a great CEO.

Many organizations use *personality tests* for evaluating and developing employees. As long as these
tests are used to indicate behavior *preferences* or
tendencies, they can be useful. If these are used to
stereotype people, they can do more harm than
good. Look at personality test results as a way to
gauge preferences that are more likely to occur in
natural or stressful situations—not evaluations of
behaviors that have actually occurred. If personality
tests present a consistent pattern with 360° feedback,
they can be useful. If they tend to conflict with
360° feedback, I would tend to minimize their
value. The way we behave—over time and as viewed
by others—says a lot more about our leadership
potential than the way we fill out self-assessment
questionnaires.

Organizational surveys can provide an interesting
picture of the "shadow" that a leader casts over his
organization. If survey results, over time, for this
leader's organization differ from the corporate norm—
in either a positive or a negative direction—you may

learn about the type of culture that she tends to create.

Be careful how you use the *anecdotal feedback* that has been given to you about this candidate. A very common error that CEOs make in evaluating a candidate's prior behavior is overreliance on anecdotal feedback. I have seen chief executives ignore positive confidential 360° feedback from multiple sources because one of their buddies regaled them with one story of inappropriate behavior. It is fine to listen to anecdotal feedback, but always *consider the source*. Think about the motivation of the person who is sharing the feedback. Realize that even the greatest of leaders have bad days, say dumb things, and make mistakes. Don't let one event override years of systematic evidence.

As you have learned, the role of CEO is very different from the role of "almost CEO." While feedback about prior history can be very useful, ideas for the changes needed in the new position can sometimes be even more valuable!

Gathering Ideas for Success in the CEO Position

While feedback about the past is a great indicator of how the candidate has led to date, suggestions for the future can help you understand what the candidate may need to do to prepare for the next level.

My own approach to developmental coaching involves asking each preselected stakeholder three simple questions:

- What are this person's existing strengths—that will help her be a great CEO in the future?

- What are this person's developmental challenges—that he may need to overcome in order for him to be a great CEO?

- If you were this person's coach, what specific suggestions would you give her—either strategic or tactical—that, if followed, would help her become a great CEO?

Although these questions seem simple, they usually result in a dialogue that lasts from thirty to sixty minutes. I then write a summary report for the candidate and the CEO that covers key themes, without identifying specific sources.

In almost every future CEO summary, the strengths highlight attributes that are requirements for even being considered. For example, almost every candidate who I have met is perceived as being extremely bright. Despite what we read in the press, stupid people are not considered for CEO positions in major corporations. Basic intelligence is considered a given for the job. If the person is not perceived as extremely intelligent, coaching will not help.

CEO candidates have a history of achieving results. If they didn't achieve results, why would they even be considered for the top job? They are almost all extremely dedicated and committed to the success of their organizations. They care about the company and its customers.

Like intelligence, hard work, and commitment, integrity should be a given. How many integrity violations does it take to ruin the reputation of even the best company? One! Executives who commit integrity violations should not be considered for the top job. In fact, they shouldn't even be coached. They should be fired!

On the areas-for-improvement side of the summary, most comments relate to interpersonal behavior. Some of the most common challenges of future CEOs are behaviors such as winning too much, adding too much value, not letting go, not being open to differing opinions, not listening, and not developing people.

As we have discussed, at the chief executive level, behavior matters. It doesn't matter a little more than behavior at the "next level down." It matters a lot more.

Every company that I have worked with has corporate values. The CEO, as much as possible, needs to be the role model and example of these values. While no human can live our values all of the time, the CEO needs to live the values as much as possible—and needs to work on making corrections when his behavior is inconsistent with the values that he is preaching to others. CEOs need to walk the talk.

As the coach for the next CEO, you need to determine, along with your successor, what changes need to be made in order for her to be the role model that your company deserves.

In review summaries of specific suggestions, I often find that the little things impact the big things. For example, some candidates may be in the habit of reading messages on their cell phones while other people are trying to talk with them. While the candidate may not intend this behavior to be rude or disrespectful, this behavior is usually viewed as disrespectful by the people who are trying to communicate. One candidate actually had sidebar conversations in board meetings while board members were speaking! Although he didn't realize how much this behavior annoyed the board members, everyone else in the boardroom did!

After you have gathered feedback about the past and suggestions for the future, it is time to figure out what your candidate needs to change—and to begin the change process.

When Coaching Your Successor, Stop and Look at Yourself!

Now that feedback has been collected and ideas for change have been generated, it is time to begin the coaching process. But before you begin coaching your successor, it is good to be aware of common problems that CEOs exhibit that limit their effectiveness as coaches. Who knows? It is possible that even you may be subject to some of these problems!

Why Doesn't She Act Like Me?

As a rule, successful human beings tend to overweight our own strengths—and underweight our own weaknesses when evaluating others. The more successful we become, the more we can fall into the *superstition trap*, which, simply stated, is, "I behave this way. I am a successful CEO. Therefore, I must be a successful CEO because I behave this way!"

You, like all successful CEOs and all successful human beings, are successful *because of* many positive qualities and *in spite of* some behavior that needs improvement.

Take a hard look at your own strengths and challenges. Realize that you may have a natural tendency to forgive even large errors that resemble your weaknesses and to punish even small flaws that occur in your area of strength.

One CEO who I admired had about the best verbal communication skills that I have ever seen. His communication skills were not just strong—they were amazing. He could "work the room" like Bill Clinton and give a speech like Martin Luther King. His successor was actually better at strategy and marketing than he was. His successor was also much better at providing honest feedback. While his successor had very strong communication skills, they were never "good enough" for the CEO—since they were not as good as his! Unfortunately, this chief executive could never accept his successor. Finally, the board had to intervene: it forced the CEO to leave and appointed his successor. The successor turned out to be a fine CEO—just a different CEO from his predecessor.

What could have been a very positive succession turned out to be an unfortunate embarrassment for the previous CEO. Don't let this happen to you!

Why Doesn't She Think Like Me?

It is hard for successful CEOs not to believe that *their* strategic thinking is the *right* strategic thinking. As you proceed in the succession-coaching process, you are going to have to let go. It can be very hard to watch your successor make decisions that are different from yours. It is especially tough since as long as you are still the CEO, you have the power to reverse the decisions.

Your successor is going to manage the organization in the future—not you. As hard as it may be, you have to let her begin to make a bigger and bigger difference.

Ego can get in the way. In one succession case, the CEO was determined that the company should go it alone and not merge with a rival (whose CEO he couldn't stand). His chosen successor finally began to feel his oats and pushed for a merger with the board. The board agreed with the successor. Rather than managing the change with dignity, the CEO resigned in a fit of anger. Don't let that happen to you!

Why Doesn't He Love My Friends?

We all tend to overvalue input from people we personally like and respect—and undervalue people we don't love as much. Face the fact that your successor may have different personal preferences from yours. Your trusted advisers may not be his.

After the transition occurs, some of your friends will actually lose status or power—and may end up leaving the company. This is tough—both for them and for you!

One of my CEO clients reported that his good friend had provided negative examples of behavior on the part of his successor. I countered that the huge majority of coworkers were reporting very positive behavior when they evaluated the same person. The CEO reflected and realized that his friend did not want the successor to get the job—for personal reasons more than business reasons. He realized that his friend was never going to give the successor a fair chance. As he was leaving the company, he convinced his friend to leave as well—so that his successor could start with a clean slate. Do let this happen to you!

Setting Developmental Goals

After you have gathered feedback and suggestions and looked in the mirror for your own potential bias, it is time to start the process of coaching your successor.

Take all of the time that you need to have an honest, heart-to-heart session. Assure him that your goal is to help him succeed—not to watch him fail. Let him know how much you believe that he has the potential to be a great CEO. Hopefully, to become a better CEO than you! Share all that you have learned and discuss all that he has learned in the process of reviewing feedback and analyzing suggestions.

Prioritize. Work together to determine the key areas for behavior change that will lead to the maximum positive relationships with key stakeholders. In many cases, behavior that needs to be changed is very consistent in all groups. For example, almost everyone may agree that your successor needs to be a better listener. In other cases, behavioral change may need to be tailored to the stakeholder group. For example, peers may feel that your successor is too assertive, while board members report that he is not assertive enough.

The goal-setting process needs to end with clear, desired outcomes. Your successor agrees to do a great job of demonstrating agreed-upon behavior as judged by agreed-upon stakeholders. The long-run goal is simple. Your successor needs to successfully develop the skills—and build the relationships— needed to make him a great CEO.

In some cases, you, as a coach, may feel a little hypocritical. You may be asking him to do some things that you haven't done very well yourself! There are two ways you can deal with this potential problem: (1) let him know that not only are you going to try to help him improve, you are going to ask him to help you improve; and (2) reinforce the desire for him to be an even better CEO than you have been!

In setting goals, show some flexibility. If his words for desired change are almost the same as yours, go with his. On the other hand, stand firm on the big issues that you believe he needs to tackle.

At the end of the goal-setting meeting, get his sincere commitment to change. Ask yourself a tough question: "Is he 'for real'?"

If your successor needs to change behavior in order to develop better relationships with key stakeholders, if he is willing to try, and if he is given a fair chance, I will share a process that can help you become the coach—who helps him achieve positive, lasting change.

Involving Key Stakeholders in the Coaching Process

The next step in the coaching process involves your successor having one-on-one conversations with each of her key stakeholders. In these conversations, she will need to:

- *Thank them for participating in the coaching process*. Take the time to acknowledge the

value of their time. Express gratitude for
their input.

- *Review strengths.* Personally commit to
continued effort in these areas of strength,
and express gratitude for the positive
recognition.

- *Openly discuss desired areas for development.*
Sincerely apologize for any mistakes that
may have damaged the relationship in the
past, and commit to improve.

- *Solicit ideas for the future.* Ask for specific suggestions that can help ensure her improvement
in targeted areas for change as well as general
suggestions that can help in her journey to
becoming a great CEO.

- *Make realistic commitments.* Avoid overpromis-
ing. Commit to listen to all ideas, consider
every suggestion, and make a good faith
effort to do the best she can to improve.

- *Ask for their continued support.* Let them
know that she plans to follow up and get
ongoing ideas for suggestions. Communicate
that positive, lasting change is a process—not
a program.

In preparing key stakeholders for the coaching process, you, as the CEO, need to encourage them to be honest, positive, and supportive in helping your successor prepare for the next role. You need to encourage them to focus more on *helping* your successor improve than on *judging* her behavior. Finally, you should point out that relationship building is a two-way street. Encourage them to focus on their own behavior—and to do whatever they can to build the relationship in a positive way.

Being a Coach-Facilitator, Not a "Coach-Expert"

The next step in the process is easy to understand, but hard to do. You need to facilitate the coaching process so that most of what is learned is coming from the key stakeholders—not from you. This can be tough for a hard-charging CEO who is used to being the boss!

After your successor has had a one-on-one dialogue with each key stakeholder, have a simple discussion that answers the following questions:

1. Who did you talk to?

2. What did you learn?

3. What are you going to do about it?

Assure your successor that you don't expect him to act on every suggestion from every stakeholder. Acknowledge the fact that some stakeholders may have their own agenda—and may be providing input aimed at helping them achieve their own personal goals. This is just part of corporate life. Help him sort the wheat from the chaff.

As you talk with your successor, he will probably have a tendency to ask you what *you* think he should do next. This is only natural. You are the CEO and he is used to reporting to you. Fight the urge to give lots of direct suggestions. Remind him that you are going to be leaving and that many of the key stakeholders are going to be remaining. He needs to build great working relationships with *them*—not with you.

The greatest challenge in behavioral change is not *knowing* what to do—the greatest challenge is doing it! Focus most of your input on helping ensure that he actually acts on the ideas that both of you feel make sense.

As a coach-facilitator, you have a simple mission. Your mission is to help your successor achieve positive, lasting change in the behavior that is most important—as judged by the people who are most important. The success or failure of your coaching will not be determined by you—or by your successor. It will be determined by the key stakeholders who interact with your successor—after you leave the organization.

Of all of the clients who I have ever coached, the client who I spent the least amount of time with improved the most! And he was great to start with. When I asked him, "What can I learn about coaching from you?" he wisely replied, "This coaching process was never about *you*. It was about me and the great people in my team. Don't make the focus on you. Make the focus on your clients." He went on to make a comment that helped me understand why he is such a great leader. He smiled and said, "I manage tens of thousands of people. Every day that I come to work I remind myself, 'Leadership is not about me. It is all about them.'"

If you want to be a great coach for your successor, make the coaching process all about him and his key stakeholders—not about you.

Follow-up Is Everything

By far, the most important variable in helping your successor achieve positive, lasting change is follow-up. And the most important follow-up is not *you* following up with her; it is *her* following up with her key stakeholders.

My partner, Howard Morgan, and I did extensive research on leadership development that involved more than 86,000 participants from eight major corporations ("Leadership Is a Contact Sport," *Strategy + Business*, Fall 2004). Our findings are almost impossible to dispute. When leaders (at all levels) receive 360° feedback, discuss what they learned with key stakeholders (as has been outlined), and consistently follow up with key stakeholders over time, they are invariably perceived as substantially improving in their selected areas for development, and they are also perceived as becoming dramatically more effective leaders. Leaders who did no follow-up with key stakeholders were seen as improving no more than by random chance.

What does follow-up sound like? Your successor needs to have ongoing dialogues with each key stakeholder. In these ongoing dialogues, she needs to discuss her specific areas for development and ask for ongoing suggestions for future improvement. The asking part of follow-up may sound something like this: "Last month I said that I wanted to become a more effective listener. As a result of my behavior in the past month, what ideas would you have for me that could help me become an even better listener next month?"

What is your role in the follow-up process? You, as the CEO coach-facilitator, need to have ongoing dialogues that reinforce "Who did you talk with?" "What did you learn?" and "What are you going to do about it?"

Your role is similar to the role of a personal trainer. You need to encourage your successor to stick with the plan, keep focused on positive change, and keep following up with key stakeholders.

Just as in getting in shape, while you may be the trainer, *she* needs to go on the diet and do the exercise. Your successor needs to understand that you will do all you can to facilitate her positive change. She will need to do the work to achieve positive change and build key stakeholder relationships.

PART IV

Passing the Baton

7 Making a Great Exit

At some point in the succession process, your successor will need to know that he is the "chosen one" who is being groomed to replace you. There is no magic formula to determine the right time.

In one case, the successor was chosen three years in advance. Everyone in the company knew who was going to be the leader and had time to adjust to the process. Although this case was a success, I would not recommend it for every company.

In another case, the successor was part of a three-person "horse race" and was notified very shortly before becoming the CEO. Although this case was a success, I would not recommend it in all cases.

Although each situation is unique, there are some common factors to consider when you are making this choice.

Letting Your Successor Know
He Is Your Successor

A key variable in making this decision is to know how many viable candidates are available who can potentially be developed for the job when you, the CEO, decide to leave. If multiple candidates are available, all are potentially qualified, and more data can help in making the right decision, waiting can definitely be in order. If a clear front-runner is known, no other internal candidates are close, and the person may well leave if not being assured of succession, then waiting can be a mistake.

After determining *when* your successor knows he is the chosen one, you will need to determine *how* to break the news to his colleagues.

From my experience, you may well be amazed at how many of your executives thought that *they* had a realistic chance at the top job! We all tend to believe what we want to believe. Although you, as the CEO, may have thought that you were sending clear and unambiguous signals concerning an executive's future opportunities, you cannot assume that he was receiving the messages that you were sending!

When your successor learns about his selection, you should coach him on how to deal with each key stakeholder—on an individual basis. Some will be thrilled with the news, some hopeful, some threatened, some angry, and some disappointed. Go through a role-playing exercise where he discusses his appointment with each person. Give him your best advice in cases where you can guess their reaction better than he can.

Before your successor talks with each stakeholder, you, as the CEO, need to have a one-on-one conversation with each person. You need to be sensitive to their emotional reaction to this news. At some point in time, after the final decision has been made, you will need to let them know that the final decision has been made. You will need to do whatever you can to encourage them to work with your successor in a way that is in the best interest of the company. In some cases, you need to be ready for their anger, their disappointment, or even their decision to leave the company.

Finally, you, as the CEO, need to avoid the "buyer's remorse" that is too common in the transition process. Once the final commitment is made, let it go. Realize that you will probably have second thoughts, but that these second thoughts do not have to be verbalized to key stakeholders. Do whatever you can to minimize your own ego—and maximize your successor's chances for a positive transition.

Declaring Victory

At a certain point in the developmental process, you, as a CEO, need to make peace with the fact that your successor—though not perfect—is good enough.

If your successor needs to develop in terms of behavioral change, if she is given a fair chance, and if she follows the steps that have been described in this memo, she will become a more effective leader, have better relationships with key stakeholders, and be better prepared to become a great chief executive.

Who should get all of the credit for the positive change in your successor?

You? You should ask for absolutely no credit. In fact, you should suggest that your successor not credit you for ideas in the entire coaching process. If she ever even mentions, "The CEO said . . .," it could imply a lack of ownership on her part—and a desire to just please you to get ahead.

Your successor? She should take absolutely no credit for her positive change and increased leadership effectiveness.

The key stakeholders? Both you and your successor should thank the key stakeholders for helping her succeed. They deserve it! The key stakeholders are the people who provided the feedback that helped your successor determine what to improve. The key

stakeholders provided ongoing ideas and suggestions. The key stakeholders were supportive and gave
your successor a chance. They deserve all of the
credit.

By giving key stakeholders all credit for her personal improvement, your successor will begin her leg
of the CEO relay race on a positive note. She has
already been handed the baton. She has already been
selected as the runner who is chosen to lead the
team. She doesn't need to prove she is great. She
needs to make them great! She doesn't need to take
credit. She needs to give credit!

Making a Great Exit!

When your successor is ready to move into the role
of CEO, you need to be ready to do something that
can be even more difficult—you need to leave!

You will be tempted by board members to stay on
the board or perhaps become the "non–executive
chairman." If you really want your successor to be
the CEO, fight this temptation. I know of a few cases
where this model has worked well. It usually doesn't!

I don't have to mention names. You know a long
list of former chief executives who developed their
successor and passed the baton—until hard times hit
the company. Then—although they allegedly didn't

want to—they "felt the call" to replace their successor and had to return to "save" the company. This "comeback" phenomenon is especially likely to occur if you are either the founder of the company or the person largely credited with the company's success.

If you really don't want to leave—stay! Staying on as CEO is not immoral, illegal, or unethical. If you want to stay, and the company can benefit from your staying, knock yourself out! Go for it as long as you can. Be honest with yourself. Just ignore this book and skip the whole "develop your successor" thing.

One of the greatest examples of CEO succession that I know involved a CEO who actually left *before* he was scheduled to go. His successor was highly sought after, and as a sign of his true commitment to succession, he left the company early so his successor would know the job was his. This showed some real leadership!

In terms of staying, no matter how great you are, you are going to have to leave sometime. We all get old—and we all die.

My final suggestion is, show some class on the way out. Do whatever you can to make your successor a winner. Get over your own ego.

Try to avoid the "return from the grave" syndrome that is becoming far too common for CEOs. For example, don't talk to the press—in a disparaging way—about your successor. Don't fall into the trap of babbling on about "what I would have done" if one of your successor's ideas fails. You would not have wanted your predecessor to have done this to you—don't do it to your successor!

Even if other people don't know what you have done, your successor will. And more importantly, you will.

If all goes well, you may have taught your successor a great lesson: how to successfully pass the baton of leadership on to her successor, who will then lead an organization that will continue to prosper in the future—an organization that all three of you will be proud of!

About the Author

Marshall Goldsmith is a world authority in helping successful leaders achieve positive, lasting change in behavior—for themselves, their people, and their teams. Marshall is the *New York Times* bestselling author or coeditor of twenty-four books, including *What Got You Here Won't Get You There*, the Harold Longman Award—Best Business Book of 2007. His major professional acknowledgments include the American Management Association—fifty great thinkers who have most impacted the field of management over the past eighty years; National Academy of Human Resources—Fellow (highest U.S. HR award); the *Times* (London)—fifty most influential living business thinkers; *BusinessWeek*—most influential practitioners in their history of leadership development; the *Economist*—most credible advisers in the new era of business; the *Wall Street Journal*—ten top executive educators; *Forbes*—five most-respected executive coaches; and *Fast Company*—America's preeminent executive coach. He is the cofounder of

About the Author

Marshall Goldsmith Partners. In 2006, Alliant International University named its schools of business and organizational psychology the Marshall Goldsmith School of Management. He is one of the few executive advisers who have been asked to work with over one hundred major CEOs and their management teams. His weekly columns appear on BusinessWeek.com and HarvardBusiness.org. Almost all of Marshall's articles, videos, and audios are available online at www.MarshallGoldsmithLibrary. com. He can be reached at Marshall@MarshallGoldsmith.com.